AMAZING
Grace

Thomas Kruger (signature)

THOMAS KRUGER (THE POET)

ISBN 978-1-64114-646-3 (Paperback)
ISBN 978-1-64114-647-0 (Digital)

Copyright © 2017 by Thomas Kruger (The Poet)
All rights reserved. No part of this publication may be reproduced, distributed, or transmitted in any form or by any means, including photocopying, recording, or other electronic or mechanical methods without the prior written permission of the publisher. For permission requests, solicit the publisher via the address below.

Christian Faith Publishing, Inc.
296 Chestnut Street
Meadville, PA 16335
www.christianfaithpublishing.com

Printed in the United States of America

JESUS LOVES ME

I ask my Lord
Why do we have to go through that valley?
And he said: the same reason the chicken crossed the road
I said: Lord, are you josh'n me?
And he said: even though I am the Lord
I still have a sense of humor,
The chicken crossed the road to get to the other side
And that's exactly what you've got to do
Everyone must go through the valley
Hang on to saving grace hold on tight with all your might,
And I'll lift you out of that dark valley
And into everlasting light
I loved you with all that I am
I took your sins to the cross, and I died for you,
Don't ever slide back into your old ways
I know that in your heart, you love me too
Love conquers all evil
Love surpasses all the other commandments,
Love your neighbor as yourself
And you will do well in every mission that you are heavenly sent
Keep on writing
This is your heavenly calling,
Keep on writing and witnessing
And know that I will always be there to keep you from falling
You are a dear and precious soul
And I love you with all that I am,
And I know that deep down that you love me too
And rest assured, I will never let go of your hand

OH TO BE FOREVER LORD WITH THEE

I had just turned forty
And I knew that newness of life was about to begin,
As I walked up to that altar of grace
And invited the Lord of Life to come in
God gave me a special gift that day
Of which to praise his holy name,
Poems of inspiration flowed over my soul
As the poetic verses came to mind to spread his glory and fame
In the years to follow
He kept me alive through many interventions,
And praise the Lord
He took upon himself the punishment for all my past sins
He nailed them to that cruel tree
No more to be remembered of,
He became the sacrificial lamb
And to me he became the purest of all love
Jesus rose triumphant over the grave
Filling us with the hope one day soon we too shall rise,
We look to the heavens from whence our help shall come
As Jesus comes to take us home, our heavenly home, somewhere beyond the skies
Before that day, we know without a doubt
That your invitation of life will reach the ends of the earth,
I thank you again for Calvary
Your undeniable proof of what you think a soul is worth
Thank you again for the victory
Thank you for your love with which you reached out to me,
I will thank you forever, and ever, and ever
For setting my soul free, as I rise up, O Lord Jesus, to be forever with thee

What Life Is All About

The world, the flesh, and the devil
Are barriers that come between us and Christ,
The lust of the eyes, the lust of the flesh, and the pride of life
Are all darkness overshadowing the light
Do a little two-step for Jesus
Dancing out into the light,
Stay out of the shadows
Those places that lead to the eternal darkness of night
Black is Satan's favorite color
And of all who follow him into hell,
White is Jesus's color
And all those who can say that all with their soul is well
Gray is a mediocre color
The color of a lukewarm Christian,
Come on, come on, stoke that fire for Christ
And wherever that you go, be a shining light of a witness for him
We are God's witnesses to the ends of the earth
We have been entrusted with God's Living Word,
We are God's laborers for the harvest to come
Through us the gospel message is either read or heard
Let that flame within you burn
Reach out and warm the coldest, hardest heart,
And may your witness be likened unto a branding iron
Permanently sealing the word in every living part
With no more darkness ruling the heart
Let's let Jesus's heavenly light shine out,
As he fills every nook and cranny of our being with his words of life
May we continue to let others know what life is truly all about

Sweet By and By

It will be worth it all
When we see Jesus,
When we rise up to be with him
Shedding these bodies of ashes and dust
The light of heaven
Will put a smile upon your face,
O what a wondrous glory awaits
All those who are saved by his loving grace
Jesus paid it all
For us his all he gave,
We shall forever praise the holy name
Of the one who arose triumphant over the grave
The only way to heaven
Is through the cross of Christ,
The blood of the Lamb of God
Is the gateway to heaven and eternal life
The spirit says come
Come, that your name may be found written upon life eternal's scroll,
Come, be baptized in the name of Jesus Christ
And accept his shed blood to wash away the sins from your soul
The invitation has gone out
Out to the very ends of the earth,
Come and receive a new heart
Come and experience the miracle of the new birth
Oh, what a day of rejoicing that will be
When the holy angels appear on high,
And we rise to meet our Lord at the sound of the victory cry
To be with him forever, forever in that sweet by and by

Hand in Hand

If you have fallen off the horse
Get right back in the saddle again,
Confess and forsake your failings
Of being drawn back into sin
God forgives
All those who ask for his forgiveness,
He said that he would never leave or forsake you
Pray that he draw you back again
Enticing you to sin
Is Satan's greatest ploy to grasp hold of your soul,
To take you out of Jesus's nail-pierced hands
It's his devious plan and uttermost goal
He doesn't want you, he doesn't love you
He just wants to draw you down with him,
He knows that the lake of fire awaits him and his followers
And for all that he can draw down to hell with him
Apply the blood of Jesus
To the doorposts of your heart,
Before the death angel comes to take you away
Jesus has done everything that he could, now you must do your part
Stay clear of the dark places
Where sin can entice you in,
Keep Jesus ever near
And he will draw you far away from the devil's den
Walk the pathways of light
That lead upward to the Promised Land,
Walk in those long-ago footprints of Jesus in the sand
All the way to the Promised Land, with Jesus hand in hand

Say Yes

Say yes to Jesus
Say yes to the Trinity's salvation plan,
Jesus says come
Come and take hold of my outstretched hand
His invitation has gone out
Out to the four corners of the earth,
Searching for those who desire a new beginning
Searching for those in need of the new birth
Born again
With death being transformed into life without end,
Born again
Crossing over into the light that never grows dim
Filled with hope
Filled and ready for the transition,
The putting off of the flesh
Making ready for that glorious flight of ascension
A body, a spiritual body
A body of light clothed in white,
Transformed at the coming of Jesus
And made ready for that upward flight
Oh, to be fully covered and filled with Christ's glory
The glory of heaven's light from above,
Oh, and to be filled with joy and peace
Overflowing with Jesus's love
We have a home up there in Glory Land
A home that Christ's hands have made,
A forever home with the Trinity of God and the holy angels
Filled with a hope that will never fade

The Spirit Is Calling

Lord, only you can put the joy in one's heart
With a love that's true and unshakable,
Your presence brings peace upon the soul
And there is nothing for you that is impossible
You created and placed the stars in the heavens
You said, "Let there be light," and there was light,
You right the wrongs, you place in the hearts the songs and
You have become every born again soul's delight
O Lord, be thou forever by our side
And in our heart and soul therein we pray for you to forever abide,
May all our lives be filled and shared with others of your loving grace
And that we of the gifts you've given may spread your glory
Throughout the whole of the world wide
Keep us Lord from falling O Lord
Keep us in the center of thy will,
May we never lose faith
And of our troubled hearts may we always say: peace be still
O Lord we live in the blessed hope
Of being in heaven one day with you,
We look to the heavens from which our help shall come
When all that you ever promised will come true
May the gifts that you have given to us
Draw others to the cross of Christ,
I pray that the Lord of the harvest
Will send more laborers to share his message of eternal life
The spirit is calling
Come home, all ye who are heavy laden,
Believe, repent, and reach out and receive
Open your heart's door and invite the Lord of Life to come in

WHERE THE RAINBOW NEVER FADES

There is a place where there is no sun
And yet there are no shadows or darkness,
A place that is neither hot nor cold
It is the place where the redeemed enter into God's rest
Therein we shall walk upon the emerald sea
The emerald sea shining like shimmering glass,
And there shall be no remembrance of the evils of that world where we once lived
It shall be a forgotten past
We shall dwell in ivory palaces
And drink from the river of life,
We shall eat of the fruits of the tree of life
And sing with the angels of unending praises to Jesus Christ
With loved ones who have gone on before
We shall walk those streets of transparent gold,
Peace, joy, and love shall be the substance
That shall replace these worn-out bodies of old
Songs of praise shall never cease
In this place that Jesus went to prepare for us,
God clothes us with robes of white and crowns of gold
And with spiritual bodies he replaces those of ashes and dust
Oh, the joys that awaitw
In that sweet by and by,
As we fly away beyond this present world
To that place of uncloudy sky
Where the hallelujahs never cease
And our new names are written in stone,
Where the rainbow never fades
Shining on forever over Our Father's hallowed throne

> To God be the glory

MEMORIES

Our lives are but passing memories
Memories in others' heart songs,
Memories, beautiful memories
Long after we are gone
Life is more than just a passing moment, and then it's gone
It is reaching out to the world that surrounds us,
It is the loving of others, the fulfilling of every law God has ever given
Faithfully walking in the light and sharing the love and light of Jesus
If others can see Jesus in us
If they can see him in our gifts that he has given,
And if they can see him in all that we say and do
Dear brothers and sisters, this is what we call Christian living
If we stand out from the crowd
If we stand up for that which we believe,
If Jesus is honored and lifted up in our hearts
Others will be more likely to open their hearts to receive
To receive the everlasting joy
To receive the hope of a better tomorrow,
To receive the love of Jesus
To receive that world beyond this world of sorrow
Yes! Memories are all that we are when we leave this world
Memories that linger on in others' hearts and minds
Memories that are passed down through the generations
Memories in the hearts of all those that we leave behind
May we, as we live, touch the hearts and souls among the living
With beautiful memories to be carried over into eternity,
And may those memories that we leave behind draw others to Jesus
That they may be victoriously and triumphantly and forever be set free

Sweet Song of the Heart

We pray for our loved ones who are saved
That they would never stray or fall away,
And we pray for those that are not saved
That they would give their heart to you one day
Come and walk the hallelujah trail with us
Come and receive of the One who for you his all he gave,
From heaven to earth he came
That at the foot of the cross your sins he may cast away
Our Father in Heaven so loved the world
That he gave his only begotten son to be the sacrificial lamb,
Come walk the hallelujah trail with us
For Christ and his sacrifice make your stand
Death could not hold him
He rose to life again,
Conquering forever death
And the consequences of sin
Everyone who puts their trust in the Lamb of God
And of whose promises never fail,
Know that those stripes and crown of thorns was ours to bear
And also that old rugged cross and every piercing nail
Every sin that kept us from Christ's everlasting glory
Are forgiven and forgotten when we open our hearts to him,
We will praise him now and forever for that old rugged cross
For no greater love could he have ever given,
I've got a home in glory land
Oh, what a sweet song of the heart that is
Oh, what everlasting joy awaits
Just knowing that one day he will take us to where he lives

The Invitation

No prettier sight shall I ever hope to see
Than that place that Jesus went to prepare for you and me,
Everything covered in sparkling gold, radiantly glowing in the light of the Son of God
And the majestic glistening of the crystal emerald sea
And of those of us who could never carry a tune before
We will sing with voices as of the angels on high,
With harps a-ring'n and with praises of singing
We will lift up our voices in that land beyond the sky
We will sing forth with the joy that God has placed within our hearts
The joy of our Savior and Lord,
And in the brotherhood of Jesus
We will lift up our voices in praises with one accord
Oh, for the joy of the greeting of loved ones again
Of walking with Jesus hand in hand,
Of heaven opening up its treasures before us
As we walk those golden paths of God's breathtaking wonderland
Heaven lies just beyond this world
And when the roll is called up yonder, praise God, I'll be there,
Come and sing those gospel songs of old with praise
With the angels and all those whom Jesus took their sins to bear
How can you neglect so great a salvation?
His word has gone out
To every corner in every nation
With love unspeakable and full of glory he reaches out his hand
Won't you put your hand in his?
If the Holy Spirit is calling out your name
This is one invitation you do not want to miss

Gifts of the Spirit

There are many ways for us to praise our Lord
Many talents and gifts of the spirit,
There are preachers, teachers, and evangelists
Of the Word of God, there are so many ways to see and to hear it
The spirit has blessed us, each and every one
Blessed us all in different ways,
And of those blessings and gifts that he has given
We are to put to use, giving to him all the glory and the praise
We must not neglect these gifts
Play those musical instruments, sing, read, write,
Spread the gospel message
Share God's heavenly light
Witness to others
Of what God has done for you,
Share your blessings
That others may see him in you
Become a beacon of light
In this dark and dreary land,
You are saved by grace
Restore that fire for Jesus back to where you first began
Knock on doors
Invite your neighbors and friends to your place of worship,
Share your joy for Jesus
And pray for souls to be loosed from sin and Satan's grip
Use those God-given talents
To draw others to the altar of grace,
And pray for God's increase to your efforts
That he may remove all obstacles along the way that you face

A Message from Heaven

God says: I don't care what you can't
I only care what you can,
And as a laborer for Christ
For you I have a plan
I gave you the gift of the pen
Of which to write,
I have given you this gift
To create verses of poems of light
You have not failed that mission
To use this gift I've given,
And I will bless you even more
Throughout this mortal life you're living
Of my message to the lost
I'll never cease to bless you,
I don't care what you can't
Just keep on doing what you do
I'll give you the messages
Of which to write down,
And those words of heavenly light
I'll bless to more and more abound
Of this gift I gave to you
I will not repent,
This gift sent down from heaven
From my hands were lovingly sent
There is no end to what you can do,
In heaven I have reserved a special place
A special place just for you

The Day of Rejoicing

A Mother's Day Poem

With love our mother raised us to the best of her abilities
Up and until that day that we were fully grown,
Now she's waiting on that other shore
To one day welcome us home
She taught us our night prayers
And of table manners too,
She taught us right from wrong
And of the things that we ought to do
The most precious thing she taught us
Was to love one another.
And that we are the most precious gift from God
That he could have ever given to a mother
Our mothers
Who now from this earth are gone,
Will always be our mothers
And will always and forever be our sweet, sweet song
She spanked us when we needed it
Corrected us when we done wrong,
And we miss her ever so dearly
Now that she is gone
One day, dear Mother
We're going to rise up to be with you,
We miss you so much
And I know that you miss us too
Upon that other shore
Our mothers patiently await,
In anxious anticipation of that day
That we walk through those pearly gates

In God We Trust

Our nation is a free nation
Because it is in God that we trust,
And our soldiers, because of their love of God and country
Know that to defend this freedom we must
Wars will never cease to be
Till Jesus comes,
And we are going to lose many,
Many more of our daughters and our sons
We lift up to heaven our thanks
To those who gave their lives to defend this freedom land,
And for all who have ever served and are now serving
Every woman and every man
Soldiers of our freedom
Soldiers of the cross,
If we don't stand up for Jesus
One day this freedom that we now know will be lost
This good ole US of A
Will never turn their back on God-loving countries,
For as long as there is a God's green earth
We know that wars will never cease
There are countries who want to rule the world
We will fight for freedom everywhere,
We will fight on land and sea
And we will fight them in the air
Our soldiers will fight our enemies
Laying down their lives to defend this "to God be the glory" land,
We raise a salute to our fallen soldiers and all those in uniform
Every woman and every man

LIVING WATERS

I know that when I gave my life to you Lord
That you gave me a heavenly mission to fulfill,
Upon the cross you bled and died for me
And of my love for you, dear Lord, to fade or falter it never will
We desire to see and to receive
Your miracles in our lives,
And one day with the holy angels we will celebrate
With a whole lot of hallelujahs and victorious high fives
Dear Jesus
Let your love like a fountain flow over and through us,
That we may of our hearts and souls bring honor
To the one whom we have come to fully love and trust
Love, dear Jesus
You gave us love like no other could ever give,
You gave us the gift of grace on that cruel cross
And it is by grace that we shall now and forever live
We pray to always feel your presence
We pray to always know that you are there,
And we pray that you will always answer our every prayer
As we share our every joy and every burden of care
May we always drink from the living waters
May we always drink from the river of life,
May our eyes be always fixed upon you
And our hearts be filled and overflowing with your unfading heavenly light
We pray dear God that you guide the searching souls
Those who are searching in all the wrong places,
Guide those searching souls, dear Jesus
Out of the desert of life and into the living waters of your oasis

NOT A GIVEN

Tomorrow is not a given,
Today is the time that we live in
Take no thought for the morrow
Sufficient unto the day is the evil thereof,
Tomorrow shall take thoughts of the things of itself
Today we must share some Jesus love
Give a hug
Go that extra mile,
Spread some Jesus love
Share that cheerful smile
And as you walk the pathways of life
Spread some happiness along the way,
Tomorrow may never come
Live life to the fullness in the Lord
Every God-given day
This day that the Lord has made
Needs to be lived like it was your last,
Life is all too short
And all too soon you are only a memory in the past
Wake up and smell the roses
Before life is over, my friend,
Over and gone
Like the wind
Remember: our tomorrows are not a given
Precious is every breath that we take,
Spread some sunshine in your Christian walk
And may Christ be in every decision that you make

The Seeds of Grace

Keep us from falling, O Lord
Keep our hearts fixed upon things above,
Keep us in the center of thy will
Keep us in the fullness of your love
Keep us from the lust of the eyes
Keep us from the lust of the flesh,
Inspire us to keep on keeping on, no matter what befalls us
Our heart's desire is to receive of your best
There is nothing in this present world
Worth putting our eternal soul in the jeopardy of hell,
Fill our hearts with thy presence dear Lord
Assuring us that all with our soul is well
We need to feel that you are ever near
We need that closer walk with thee,
We need to know that in our heart of hearts
You are ours for eternity
There are many paths
But there is only one that leads to the Promised Land,
We follow only those that Jesus has lain before us
Declaring to the world that we have made our stand
He is the way, the only way
No other can satisfy a soul like he can,
He is the way, the truth, and the life
And for each of us whom he has called, he has a plan
In this journey of life that God has given to us
We must always follow where he leads,
Let's plant and water of the word of God and walk the talk
Caring and liberally sowing God's life-giving, life-saving,
God's precious grace's seed

WELL DONE

Jesus said
What you do unto others you do unto me,
Love your neighbor as yourself
And with my love flowing from your converted heart be all that you can be
Of that which we give away
This is the only treasure that we can take with us,
Greed and covetousness are an abomination to the Lord
Let us not build bigger barns to store our stuff
Where your treasure is
There will your heart be also,
Store up treasures in heaven
As you with the love of Jesus upon others bestow
To widows, orphans, and the poor
With a helping hand reach out,
Share Christ's love
For truly, isn't that what life is all about
Share the joy that Christ has sown in your heart
Share a meal, share a hug, share a smile,
Reach out with all that you are
Go that extra step, go that extra mile
God's eyes are upon us
Are we examples of what a Christian should be?
Or are we falling short in our walk
Of guiding others to the altar of grace to be set free?
One life is all that God gives to each of us
To be lived to the full in his son,
That he might write beside each name in the Lamb's book of life
Those two precious words: "Well done"

Glory and Honor

My desire
Is neither riches nor fame nor any other thing,
My only desire is to share the word
The glory of Jesus, the Holy of Holy's name
We must keep reaching out
Presenting the gospel to those who have never heard,
Neither by song, verse, or sermons
Of Jesus Christ, the eternal and living word
So much to do
In so very little of time,
We must with heartfelt care for others share the gospel light
And all glory of conversions to be O Lord Jesus thine
He is our living Savior
Who died and rose again,
Who willingly went to the cross for us
Taking upon himself the punishment for our sin
What he has done
We could never repay,
We are here to share the Good News
Every God-given and God-blessed day
We are to use our God given gifts and talents
To the praise of our living and loving God,
Keep the candle of your heart forever lit
While upon this God's green earth that you now tread
He is the light of heaven and earth
The eternal light that burns within,
We bestow upon him the glory and the honor
The glory and the honor that is forever due him

BEYOND THE SKY

As our life here upon earth
Fastly approaches its mortality's end,
We ponder within our hearts the river of life
And of that which awaits us beyond the next bend
Jesus knows the trials that we are going through
For he is forever there to guide us through each and every one,
As we place into the hands our every joy and care
Into those hands of our Father God's most beloved only begotten son
We have traveled this world from life's beginning to life's end
For some of us, we came to Jesus much later in life,
We thank God that we received grace through the knowledge of the truth
And stepped out of the darkness and into his marvelous light
Our hearts are now fixed and settled
Not in this world but in the next,
As the light of our lives fastly fades away
As we are about to enter into God's rest
Our hope is not in the here and now
But into that place that Jesus went to prepare for us,
As we cling fast to our nation's motto
For truly it is in God that we have placed our hope and trust
We hold fast to hope
The hope that Jesus has sealed within,
Of rising up one day to glory
To be forever and ever with him
That day when death takes hold
That day we bid this world good-bye,
When our earthen vessel is consecrated to the ground
And our spirit takes wing, rising victorious to that kingdom beyond the sky

Only through Jesus

These bodies of flesh were never meant
To last forever without decay,
For one day we shall shed them forever
As the spiritual replaces these of dust, mud, and clay
And then we are either going up
Or we are going down,
To the fiery pits of hell
Or to wear a golden crown
Life is filled with choices
We must choose wisely the paths that we take,
There are eternal consequences
To the choices that we make
We can live in this world
With our lives filled with bitterness and strife,
Or we can accept Jesus into our heart
And live in the newness of life
Life's road is not an easy one to travel
Life's consequences are according to the paths that we follow,
We can either bask in glory
Or in sorrow and self-pity continue to wallow
God has not promised us
All bright and sunny days,
For there will be clouds
And many a storm to come our way
Yes! Life is a hard pill to swallow,
And it is only through Jesus
That we can face without fear
The challenges of our every tomorrow

LIVING FOR HIM

With Jesus
The sun is always shining in our heart,
With a promise, an oh so wonderful promise
To never from us ever depart
Do not faint, grab hold of life
No matter what life throws at you,
And God in his perfect timing
Will gloriously and victoriously see you through
Take heart
In that you do not walk this world alone,
And that somewhere in heaven
The rainbow continues to shine over God's glorious throne
May the poems continue to flow through my pen
Until the day the roll is called up yonder,
And may we persevere
As upon God's Holy Word we daily ponder
There will be many a trial
In this life that we will face,
But we will overcome them all
In the joy of living in God's amazing, amazing grace
Jesus endured the cross
For the glory that was set before him,
And we must do the same
Praising God for removing all the horrors
Of the consequences of past sins
Jesus paid it all
We will continue to lift him up in songs, poems, and praise,
As we live our lives through him
The rest of our born-again God-given days

The Hands of Creation

He, whose hands
Made the worlds that be,
He whose hands healed the sick,
Raised the dead, and made the blind see
He who left his home in glory
To set us free,
He whose hands
They nailed to that cruel tree
True, the Jews are God's chosen people
But because of their unbelief,
God has opened the door for the Gentiles
To the stealing of their hearts like a thief
That coming of his triumphant return
Is steadfastly fixed in every born-again believer's heart,
To hold on to and to cling to till that day
That we, from this world of pain and suffering depart
All he has ever promised
Will be miraculously fulfilled that day,
As we take on the change, as we rise
When Christ, like a thief, comes to take us away
What a day of rejoicing that will be
When we take up wings and fly away,
Being transformed to be like him
As we are lifted up to that place of uncloudy day
Songs with the holy angels
And all those who have gone on before,
Shouting joyous hallelujahs
As we rise to be with Jesus in that place of forevermore

BLESSINGS OF THE HEART

Lord, stir within me
The gift that you have given,
That I may continue to put from pen to paper
All the poems that you inspire me to be written
Your message I pray
Be upon every written line,
All glory be to you
No glory be of mine
Yes, I am the messenger
Of the good tidings that he has given,
Blessed by God to write these verses
All the rest of the days of my living
It is a gift of heavenly light
To which I will always be true,
To bring God's words that he has given to me
In verse to bring to you
I sometimes get goose bumps
Thinking about how much by God I'm blessed,
Giving to him my all, my all of everything
As he gives to me his best
I love to write, this is my calling
God has, with this gift, blessed my soul,
I will cherish this gift all the days of my life
As I have made the writing of these poems my lifelong goal
Jesus, Blessed Redeemer
You have filled my soul with words of treasure,
Blessing my heart even more so
Than earthly fame, fortune, or pleasure

That Far-Off Shore

Part the waters, dear Lord
I'm growing old and I'm desiring to come home,
Home to that far-off shore
No more pains of aging, achy bones
Forget the manna, Lord
My soul hungers to be with you,
You are the well of living waters
Quenching all thirst like no other could ever do
You have nailed my sins to the cross
You have turned my darkness into bright, sunny days,
You have washed my soul in your shed blood
I am a sinner saved by grace
Forget me not, Lord
Chastise me when I stray,
And as I stumble through this life
I pray that you cast me not away
I am not perfect
And as I walk this earth I shall never be,
Only when I go to be with you, dear Lord
Will I from this body of sin be set free
I am a living soul
A soul different from every other,
And through God our Father, dear Jesus
I have become to you and through you a brother
Guide me along the pathways of life
Guide me until that day you come to take me home,
Home to that other shore
To that place like none other that I have ever known

TREASURES IN HEAVEN

Jesus is mine
He loves me in spite of my faults,
He took my sins to the cross
By his shed blood my soul he bought
I write to share his love
The love that took him to that old rugged cross,
Without the cross there is no redemption
And without the resurrection we would all be lost
Of Jesus and his love
We must to others share,
We must spread the Good News
And faithfully direct others into the arms of his loving care
Life is but a passing moment
Compared to that which beyond awaits,
We must prepare for eternity
Before it is forever too late
We as Christians are laborers together with God
Messengers of the Good News,
Sharing the soul-saving gospel message
Of which we must be always faithful and true
If we, in love, do our part
And never thereof to ever cease,
God will faithfully do his part
And bring about the increase
Reach out
Your days upon the earth are numbered and few,
Make drawing others to the cross your lifelong goal
And God will add to the treasures awaiting there in heaven for you

Haven of Light

The eagle, the kingfisher
The sea gull, the osprey, and the pelican,
These are fishers of fish
But the greatest of fishers are those of the souls of man
We cast out the lifeline
God's salvation message from the Bible to be heard,
We pray, we fast, and we reach out
Sharing to others the joys of God's Living Word
We are God's planters of the seeds of life
Getting souls ready for the upcoming harvest,
And of all our efforts we put forth in his name
He does faithfully bless
Fishers of men
We are like farmers in a way,
Planting and watering
Till he comes to take us away
The Word of God
Is the seeds that we sow,
Sprinkled with living waters
We watch what we planted begin through Jesus to grow
If we have led
But one soul to Christ,
That soul's worth
Is a treasure without price
Cast out the lifeline
To those drowning in the sea of life
Cast out the lifeline
And draw others out of the darkness
Into God's glorious haven of heavenly light

My Jesus

Do I know Jesus?
Oh how I know Jesus,
Savior, Creator, Friend, and Lord
Oh how I know Jesus
I hold him close
Close to my heart,
He is my every reason for living
He has from this world set me apart
He is the creator of all things
Creator of the stars, the heavens, and the earth,
He is the second person of the Holy Trinity
He is the Christ child of the virgin birth
He is the creator, the creator of everything in the whole vast universe,
He is, he was, and he shall always be
The one whom I now write praises in verse
With the gift that he has given to me
He is in my every waking moment
He is the creator and savior of my soul,
He walks and talks with me
And leads me in the paths that I should go
Do I know Jesus?
He lives within my heart,
Do I love Jesus?
No one or anything can tear us apart
He is always near
He is the way, the truth, and the life, he is the seeker,
He is the living word, the Lord of Lords, and King of Kings
And for all those that are written in the book of life
He is the soul keeper

Wings as Eagles

I know that we will face many trials
Before our lives on earth are done,
But we will face them all in triumph and victory
In our knowledge and trust of our Father God's only begotten son
When we were born again
When we gave our hearts to him,
When we were washed in the blood
When we opened our heart's door and invited the Lord of Life to come in
That day changed everything
As we gave our all to him,
We experienced the cleansing flood
As the blood of the cross washed away our sin
He gave us a new heart
In which to worship him,
His love like a warm covering draped over our soul
In an everlasting love without end
We now walk the upward paths
The straight and narrow ways,
We will continue to walk them all our earthly days
Until our lives on earth wither and fade
Only to wake up on that other shore
Where pain and sufferings are no more,
To receive of God's everlasting treasures
Of which our Lord has laid up for us in store
Oh, to sing glory and praises to Jesus with the angels on high
In that awesome place of endless days of wonder,
Taking up wings as of eagles and fly away
With joy-filled hearts to God's haven of peace up yonder

Treasures in Heaven

The only treasures here and beyond
Are those souls that we lead to Christ today,
Waiting there to rejoice with us
With showers of blessings for showing them the way
We all own things
Just don't let things own you,
Our treasures should be of our loved ones
Those here and those souls in heaven waiting there for me and for you
Those who reached out
Those who believed,
Those who accepted Christ's sacrifice
And reached out and received
These are our true treasures
These are what life is worth living and fighting for,
Thank God for Jesus's increase added to our efforts
We could not have asked for anything more
We must use our God-given gifts and talents
To draw and lead others to those pearly gates,
Where therein lie the true treasures
Of those on that other side, who for us, now awaits
Jesus walks with us today
He is with us through every temptation and trial,
He is with us as we reach out with his love in our hearts
He is with us and blesses us for going that extra mile
Our treasures should be of those we have led to Jesus
These are the treasures of the harvest that we are commissioned to reap.
Those souls whom we have led to Christ
Are the only true treasures from earth that we can hold on to in our hearts and keep

Everlasting Joy

Jesus did not come to condemn or destroy lives
He came to earth to save souls,
He came, the only begotten son of God our Father
The living sacrifice that the prophets of old had foretold
The creator of everything that we see
And of everything that we do not see,
He left his home in glory
To become the sacrificial Lamb to set souls free
Without the blood of the Lamb applied
There is no redemption of sin,
Without Jesus's sacrifice on the cross
Our future would be filled with darkness within
Reach out and take hold of those nail-pierced hands
Come to the cross and be washed in that crimson flow,
Take and plant the Word of God
And with God's blessings, watch those seeds of life blossom and grow
Yes! Jesus left his home in glory
He came to give his life a sacrifice for us,
We must accept this gift of our Father's love
As the reconciliation for we who are but ashes and dust
Christ gave his all for us
We owe our all to him,
This is the gift of unmerited favor, this is God's gift of grace
With this gift he cleanses our soul within
Reach out and take hold of God's promise of eternal life
Don't leave this world without Jesus in your heart,
Come now and share God's everlasting joy
God's everlasting joy that will never ever from your heart depart

THE VICTORY CRY

Don't be as the virgins whose lamps went out
Who waited till it was too late,
In the blinking of an eye, the Lord will come for those who are ready
Closing behind him heaven's gate
Oh, what a day of rejoicing
For all who have kept their lamps filled and burning
Always ready for that sudden appearance
And the trumpet's sound of his glorious returning
He is about to fulfill his promise of coming back to take his saints home
The dead in Christ will be the first to rise,
And then we who are saved and still alive
Will be caught up together with them to join our Lord in the skies
This will be the greatest happening to ever happen
Since the beginning of time,
Rejoicing shall echo forever throughout the halls of glory
I have made him mine, I pray that you make him thine
Come one, come all
Come to the wedding feast,
Come one, come all
From the greatest to the least
Everything is made ready
Ready for that blessed event that is about to happen,
Go tell it on the mountain
Go tell foe and friend
It is time to reach out
For your soul's sake don't let that day pass you by,
That day when the rapture of the saints takes place
That day when the archangel gives that triumphant victory cry

The Altar of Grace

God loves all
All those who have listening ears,
He listens to their troubles and their joys
And calms their every fears
Sometimes he speaks with a small wee voice
And sometimes his voice is loud and clear,
We may not always feel his presence
But nonetheless, he is always near
He will not cast out
Any who come to him,
He went to that cross for all,
All who come repenting of their sins
Forgiveness at the cross
Is full and free,
He died for all
He died for you and he died for me
He rose to life again
As we too shall rise one day,
As he lifts us up to be with him
In that long-ago foretold day of the catching away
Resurrection day is coming
Are you truly ready to meet your Maker?,
If not, get up to that altar of grace
And make your salvation sealed and sure
His nail-pierced hands
Are reaching out to draw you in,
Reach out and grasp the victory
And rid your soul of all condemnation of sin

WE WILL KNOW AS WE ARE KNOWN

He will wipe away all tears from our eyes
No tears shall ever fall on those streets of gold,
No more heat and no more cold
No more aches and pains of growing old
Singing and rejoicing
With the angels on high,
Heavenly music flowing from harps of gold
The reuniting with loved ones in that sweet by and by
Heaven is beyond all imagination
Beyond all expectations of our finite mind,
We may not know what awaits
But it will be far better than that which we leave behind
Arthritis, cancer, diabetes, Alzheimer's, poverty
All this will be no more,
Peace, joy, happiness, and hearts overflowing with praises and song
These are only a fraction of what God has in store
Oh, to converse with Jesus
And the angels that never fell,
And all the apostles, and our loved ones who died
And who are now forever alive and well
A light so bright
Where no shadow can run and hide,
Jesus, the light of heaven
Who for us was crucified
Jesus's love will flood over our soul
No more remembrance of the life that is now past,
We will know as we are known
As Jesus answers our every question before we even ask

The First Will Be Last and the Last First

Part the waters, dear Lord
I'm ready to come on home,
I've fought the good fight
And am still writing to your glory of many, many a poem
I have written a multitude of verses of light
To lift up in praise your name, dear Lord,
I have gleaned these thoughts that you have given to me
From the power of the written word, the Spirit's mighty sword
I came into the fold later in life
At forty years of age, I've finally seen the light
I was encouraged to read the story
Of the workers hired into the vineyard and worked throughout the heat of the day,
And other workers who were hired and worked but the last hour of the day
And in the end they both received the same amount of pay
As long as we are alive
There is hope until our last breath of die' n,
And of this there is a parable that I love to quote
"A live dog is better than a dead lion"
My advice is
Don't put off what you must do one day,
You never know when some drunk driver
Is going to come along and take your life away
I may have come into the fold late in life
But my wages are the same as those who came in first,
I praise God for those encouraging words
And for his son for quenching my spiritual thirst

Never Alone

Nothing on this earth or anywhere else
Can separate us from the love of Jesus,
No person or circumstance can intervene
And sever that love that Jesus has for us
He said that he would never leave or forsake us
And I believe his every spoken and written word,
And like the berreans
We search the scriptures daily for proof of that which we have heard
Being a Christian
Does not mean that troubles will not come our way,
But it does mean
That we have a direct line to our Father in Heaven when we pray
Jesus walks with us
Wherever we go,
So we keep on counting our blessings
As out of God's heart they continually flow
What a savior, our mighty God
Who made the heavens, the earth, the mountains, and the sea,
What a savior
Who knows and loves and cares for you and me
It is so hard for us to comprehend
That the God of all creation's glory,
Guides us through our life in this world
From beginning to end of our whole mortal life's story
I yearn to see my loved ones again
All those who loved the Lord and have reached that other shore,
One day I shall trade in this world's treasures of deceit
For the treasures in that awesome place where time shall be forever nevermore

Brotherly Love

I love my paternal brothers
And my brothers and sisters in Christ,
But the brother I love most
Is the one who gave me life
My life and soul belongs to him
I am his and he is mine,
I walk with him and I talk with him
No greater love could I ever find
Oh, how I love Jesus
Who took my sins to bear,
Oh, how I love Jesus
And to abide in his gentle care
I thank him for life
And for pointing me in the right direction,
And if I fail him in any way
I thank him for the chastisement of his fair and just correction
To have God living
Inside of one's soul,
Fills the heart with overwhelming joy
And gives life a new meaning, purpose, and goal
Jesus is more than a brother
He is our closest and dearest friend,
And of our mortal lives
He is the beginning and the end
And when we leave this world
To go to be with him,
We know that we have found joy eternal
And life more glorious than we could ever comprehend

Do You See What I See?

He is the God of heaven and earth
He is the God of the virgin birth,
He is the God who went to the cross
For what he deemed our soul worth
He died and rose again
Conquering forever death and sin,
He is the searcher and redeemer
Of the souls of men
We owe our all to him
He who holds the heavens in place,
It is in him and through him
That we receive his unmerited favor of the gift of grace
When I see the stars
Sparkling like diamonds, pressed deep into the dark velvet of the night,
I think of heaven
And the one whose home is glowing in everlasting light
When I see the flowering dogwoods and rosebuds bloom
I think of the one who took our sins to bear,
And when I see all the glory of his creation
I thank him for placing it all into the hands of our gentle care
I wake up every morning to the birds' sweet songs
Watching the dragonflies in flight.
And the butterflies visiting spring flowers
Of colors oh so bright
He spread the heavens like a curtain
As he looked down upon his creation of this big blue marble.
And of all the things herein and beyond
Of which we continue in awesome wonder to marvel
The dew of the morning
The cleansing smell of the rain in the air,
It all brings the senses alive
And the soul made more fully aware

The mountains, lakes, and rivers
The oceans and the seas,
The souls he placed upon this earth
And all of his beautiful creation of which he is well pleased
We cannot but praise him
For all the glory that we see,
And to think that the same God that created all this
Is the same God that created you and me
I see him through the prophets
I see him through the disciples,
I see him in the living words
Of the truth that is written in our bibles
Do you see what I see?
He is everywhere,
He is with you always
Listening to your every prayer
He will not always give you what
You want, but he will always give you what's best,
Give him your all
And let him take care of the rest
Do you see what I see?
Jesus is in every leaf upon every tree, and also in you and me,
He lives in every born-again Christian
Every repentant soul forever forgiven and set free

THE LOWLY SHEPHERDS

Of that day that we call Christmas
Our hearts wander back to that blessed event of long ago,
Whether it was in the time of harvest,
Springtime, or in the time of snow, no one seems to know
It was that miraculous event when the heavens opened up
And angels appeared in a burst of heavenly light,
It was to the lowly shepherds that they came
Oh, how that must have been a frightening but beautiful sight
The darkness that covered the night
Was suddenly filled with the light as of the day,
As the angels spoke to the shepherds of good tidings
Of a savior being born into the world that day
In a lowly manger
The Christ child was born,
No parades, no bands playing, no singing and dancing
And no blast from Gabriel's horn
It was to the lowly shepherds
That the holy angels came,
And not to the high and mighty
Of earthly scholars and kings
Wise men followed a wandering star
They came bearing gifts to present to the newborn king,
Wise men still continue to follow him
Raising their hands toward heaven singing glory to his name
The shepherds could not contain within themselves the joyful news that they had just heard
They went forth praising God with joy-filled hearts spreading the Good News,
And ever since, the word continues to spread to the ends of the earth
By all who came and are coming to the Lord,
Including all those who are converted of the Jews

The Trinity's Salvation Plan

What in this world is worth
Subjecting your soul to eternity in hell?
Life is short, my friend
And believe me, there will be a final toll of the bell
Are you ready to cross over? Are you ready for that which lies ahead?
One day all that you are shall be changed
All fleshly desires can no longer be fulfilled
That day when your physical body is pronounced dead
But if you live in Christ, if you ask him to be savior of your soul
If you renounce the desires of darkness, and have made a vow to walk in the light,
And to make sharing the gospel of Christ with others the rest of your life's goal
Your soul will feel such relief
That nowhere else in this world you could ever find,
When Jesus enters into one's heart
Two become one as, inseparable, together they bind
Our Father in Heaven, our Father God's son, and the Holy Spirit
Are the Trinity of God, the inseparable three yet one,
And when we enter into that holy circle
We are to become one with Jesus in that world yet to come
Praise God for a love beyond comprehension
Praise God for the salvation plan,
Praise God for the cross of Christ
And the Trinity's salvation plan
We can never praise him enough
We can never repay the debt that we owe,
But we can accept his offer of life without end
By believing and accepting his salvation plan for our soul

The Wages of Sin

Having Jesus in your heart
Is like having a piece of heaven grasped tightly in your hand,
As you walk that pilgrim journey
That leads to the Promised Land
Satan is like a roaring lion
Seeking whom he might devour,
He is the prince of darkness
But I declare unto you, of that one of the greater power
Satan is a defeated foe
Defeated by Christ upon the cross,
Satan shouted the victory cry when he saw Jesus die
But this turned out to be our greatest gain and Satan's greatest loss
That third day after the crucifixion
Christ rose triumphant over death and the grave,
Satan experienced his greatest defeat that day
When Christ, for us, his life he gave
The lake of fire
Is Satan's final destiny,
And all that follow him
Into that eternal burning sea
These words are written
For all those who are still among the living,
Experience the new birth through Jesus Christ
For he is the holy one of divine forgiving
Satan has his followers
Do not be found among them,
They shall receive their reward
Their reward of the wages of sin

ETERNAL TREASURES

Like what Satan desired to do to Peter
He wants to sift us like wheat,
But he has no power
Over those who have kneeled at Jesus's feet
All who come to Jesus
Need not fear,
For our Lord and Savior
Has promised to be forever near
We fear only the Lord
And whom we fear we love,
He came down to live among us
Leaving his heavenly home above
Our missionaries go to other lands
With that sword of the Lord in hand,
There is no more powerful weapon on earth
That can change the destiny of man
The Word of God
Is more powerful than the bomb, the tank, and the gun,
It can change the vilest of sinners
Into the most powerful witnesses for Jesus
When their victory at the cross is won
Jesus says come
Come to the altar of grace, my friend,
And open up your heart's door
And invite the Lord of Life to come in
You will never regret that decision
That decision of leaving your past life behind,
For the treasures that lie ahead are eternal
Far excelling all the temporal earthly treasures that you could ever find

The Bright Morning Star

Life is a journey without end
As we transform from mortality to the immortality of eternal life,
Death is not a day for tears of mourning
It is a day of rejoicing for one going to be forever with Christ
We shall know as we are known
As we unite with our loved ones again,
We will rejoice forevermore
With family and friends, amen
Listening to the angels sing
And the harp's sweet music floating in the air,
Just happy to be with Jesus
No more earthly trials to bear
We who have the voice of a croaking frog
Will outsing the nightingale,
We who could not play any instrument of music
Will play without one note to ever fail
We will dance
And never miss a beat,
We will shake a leg
With uncontrollable rhythm in our feet
We will praise our Lord
With all that we are,
Forever grateful, and forever faithful
To that bright and morning star
The river of life flows freely
As the rainbow hovers over God's throne,
We praise God for bringing us through our trials
And for opening the gates of heaven and welcoming us home

Sunny Skies of Blue

When I leave the nursing home
I leave my heart behind,
I am so in love
With that sweet, sweet, sweet wife of mine
She has had to endure so much
I don't know how much more that we can take,
We love you, Lord Jesus
But our hearts are about to break
You said that you would never put on us
More than we can bear,
I place my wife into your hands
To have and to hold in your loving care
Watch over her, dear Lord
I am past being able to do that task,
Love her, dear Lord
Is all in this world that I ask
We will continue in faith to pray for miracles
Knowing that all things are possible with you,
We pray that you remove the storm clouds that hang over us
And restore those sunny skies of blue
Oh, for those sunny skies of blue

SENSE OF HUMOR

I love you, dear Jesus
I love you with all my heart,
You've put up with a lot of my failings
But your love for me will never depart
You've saved my life and my soul
Over and over again,
Whenever I fell short, you brought me back
And cast away my sin
Of the gift that you have given to me
I'll cherish it till the day I die,
I feel like I've been overblessed
More than all the stars in the sky
Poetry was never my thing
But when I got saved, it hit me like a bolt of lightning,
And now I love the words of verse
And as long as I live I'll keep on writing
It brings joy to my heart
That you gave this blessing to me,
And I will cherish this gift always
As I write these praises in verses of thee
I like to write the funny ones too
I like to see people smile and laugh,
Laughter is the music of the soul
A sense of humor is a great blessing to have
A camel passing through the eye of the needle
Lord, that was a good one,
It's a wonderful feeling to know
That even God can pull a pun

The Sweetest Words

We look to the heavens
For the Holy of Holiest one,
We look to the heavens
For that sudden appearance of God's Son
He's coming back, you know
Coming back, and he won't be coming back alone,
He's coming back with those who have gone on before
Coming back to take us home
Holy angels will fill the heavens
Holding back the devil and his demons of darkness,
Jesus is taking us home to be with him
Taking us home to enter into our eternal home of rest
While here on earth we strive toward the mark
Desiring to hear God's "Well done,"
We look to the heavens for that blessed promise
Of the resurrection yet to come
We strive toward the mark
We strive to receive the prize that awaits us at the end,
We reach out for perfection

Perfection that can only be obtained through him
We are sinners
Saved by grace,
And we will not find perfection
Until we look full into the light of our Lord's wonderful face
We are washed in the blood
We are redeemed by Christ's sacrifice on the cross,
We all have sinned and come short of the glory of God
There is none righteous, no not one
All without Christ are lost
The Bible encourages us
To comfort one another with these words,
Jesus Christ is coming back
Are these not the sweetest words that you've ever heard?
Praise God
He's coming back for you and me,
Praise God that from these aching and decaying bodies of flesh and bone
We will be miraculously swept away and set free

Never Give Up

Give me of that which to write
I feel like I'm running dry, Lord,
Fill my pen with the Living Word
That I may wield it like a mighty sword
Let it penetrate to the heart
Let it touch and heal the soul,
These verses of light that are sown
I pray reach out and accomplish their goal
Jesus, you have given me a gift
And I have been faithful in all you have given me to do,
All glory for that gift, dear Lord
All glory be unto you
I write
I write of that which you have placed upon my heart,
For each poem I needed a seed
An inspired beginning of where to start
The dry spells, dear Lord, are very disheartening
Those dark times when the seeds do not come,
I know that I must pray always for your guidance
For all the victories yet to be won
Those victories will be won
As we reach out in faith for the prize,
Never giving up
No matter what trials upon us arise
Jesus declared unto the apostles the words
Of "O ye of little faith,"
We must never give up as we continue to run the race
Standing always firm in his most amazing, amazing grace

Let the Hallelujahs Begin

The heavens will split open
Like the day of Jesus's birth,
And the sky will be covered
With angels hovering over all the earth
Then the greatest miracle of them all will occur
The King of Kings shall suddenly appear,
As Jesus our Lord and Savior
From heaven to earth draws near
What a day
What a day of rejoicing that will be,
When our most precious Lord Jesus
In the clouds we shall see
The shout of victory
Shall fill the air,
As we are lifted up
From here to there
The graves will be opened
And the dead in Christ shall rise,
All the mysteries of life and death shall be revealed
As the lost are left behind with grieving tears in their eyes
The word has gone out

Gone out to the ends of the earth,
The Trinity's salvation plan has been fulfilled
By the holy one of the virgin birth
Born to face the cross
Born to save the lost,
Hallelujah! What a savior, what a friend we have in Jesus
Who paid salvation's cost
Out of his love for us he paid the price
That none other ever could,
He paid the price through every hammer blow
Of nails through flesh and wood
Praise God for his saving grace
And salvation at the foot of the cross,
Come receive forgiveness of sin's consequences
No searching soul needs ever to be lost
Come be washed in the blood of the Lamb
Come be washed without and within,
Come let Jesus cast out your sin
And let the hallelujahs begin
Praise the Lord

OUR MISSION

When one opens up oneself
Opening up the heart to invite Jesus to come and live within,
It is the greatest decision in their life that they will ever make
As a new and wonderful life is about to begin
With a new heart and a brand-new start
And a new path before them to walk,
And a whole new life
Filled with a whole new manner of living and talk
When people see the change that through Jesus has taken place
And all the difference he has made in your life,
And your conversion beginning to draw others to the cross
As the redemption of your soul turns from darkness into light
Jesus's goal upon that old rugged cross
Was to redeem all those who are weary and tempest tossed.
That they would find new hope flowing over their soul
In the acceptance of Christ's sacrifice to redeem all who are lost
Life without Jesus, my friends
Is a life not worth living,
A life of self-gratification
Needs to change to one of unselfish loving and giving
An encouraging word
The giving of a friendly smile,
The reaching out of a helping hand
The going with someone that extra mile
We can all do something
To make this world a better place,
With Jesus all things are possible
Let us not fail our mission of sharing God's wonderful gift of amazing saving grace

Blessed Memories

Of your gifts that God has given to you
Only you can do it best,
Reach out to others with your God-given talents
And he will reach out and add his blessings to the rest
We have a mission, you and I
And only you can do what you do,
This is why God has blessed you with this gift
It is not only a blessing unto others
But it is also a blessing unto you
Lift up your spirits
Use the gifts that he has given
And rejoice in the rewards of your gift
Throughout this life that you are now living
Blessings to your soul
Comes through reaching out to and blessing others,
Do what you do best
And lift up your praises and thankfulness to Jesus
As he brings into the fold new sisters and new brothers
Jesus is the giver of spiritual gifts
To be used to draw others to him,
To draw others to that blood-cleansing flow
That washes away every dark stain of sin
Through his gifts he has opened up a whole new world to you
These gifts were given not to only lift up one's own soul
But to lift up others as well,
This is our Lord's purpose for his gifts and his goal
Keep on keepin' on, brothers and sisters
And God will give within you a new song,
And of those lives of whom through Jesus you have blessed with your gift
You will always be among their most precious memories after you are gone

The Ringing of the Bells

I love to see good things happening in people's lives
Those things that bring joy and thanksgiving to swell up in their hearts,
Good things happen to those who make good things happen to others
Live your life as one of giving and forgiving, and never from that ever depart
A giving heart is a light shining out for Jesus for all to see
What you do unto others
Jesus says, what you do unto others you do unto me
Reach out and lovingly touch someone's heart
That it may be a blessing to you and a life-changing joy to their soul,
And do it all in the name of Jesus
For this is your mission for the accomplishing of his goal
He knows your every thought and your every need
And he knows your every unselfish good deed,
And when you come to him in faith and unite with others who have been called
To go into the fields of harvest planting the words salvation's seeds
That souls from sin may be forever and ever freed
You are his spokesperson to carry out the Good News both near and far,
You are the messengers of the good tidings of Jesus, that bright and morning star
Jesus's love is spreading
Spreading through those who have experienced it for themselves,
He is the morning star, he is the light that brightens the heaven of heavens
His message of salvation has been carried from one end of the earth to the other
And many are coming in answer to the church's ringing of the bells

Beyond the Stars

If you take the time to look around
The trials will seem much smaller in life,
As Jesus walks with us through each and every one
Knowing that at the end of the tunnel there is light
We do not face our trials alone
Jesus is with us all the way,
He promised to never leave us nor forsake us
When he came into our hearts, he came in to stay
We will not fear
Of that which the world lays before us,
For we have the God of hope watching over our souls
And it is in our Father God's son of which we have placed our trust
We will take each trial as it comes
We will take it together one day at a time,
Alice, I love you no matter what befalls us
For I am forever yours and you are forever mine
Our love for each other will see us through
Till that day that Jesus comes to take us home,
Alice, as long as I live and am able to move
You will never be left alone
We will fight the good fight
Placing ourselves and our future into Jesus's hands,
He promised never to give us more than we can bear
As we await our rising up to the Promised Land
We are yours, dear Jesus
And in our hearts you are ours,
As we await our fate upon this earth
For that day we receive our home beyond the stars

Speedy and Sally

I'm so glad
That I wrote a poem,
That reached down
And touched your funny bone
I love to see people laugh
What would this world be like without a sense of humor?
We would all dry up and blow away
And that's for doggone dad burn sure
I'm glad that Silly Sally
Touched your funny bones,
Maybe you will find another verse or two that will tickle you
Somewhere hiding within my book of poems
Speedy and Sally
You are a beautiful couple,
You two are a blessing
Of more than a cup full
United together as one
When love flooded over your soul and filled your precious heart,
Taking your vows, that nothing or no one
Could ever tear you apart
I thank God always that he gave me the gift of verse
And that something funny sometimes is created out of pen and ink,
And just like Silly Sally
It becomes a classic, at least so some do think
My gift is to keep on writing
Till the trials upon this earth are over and done,
I have a mission to touch others hearts with Jesus, joy, and laughter
Till that great and wonderful resurrection day to come

FRIENDS

When I was in school at Webster High
I had two best friends, one was Lee and the other was Jim,
We hunted, fished, and camped together
We were friends through thick and thin
After graduation
Lee moved to Wisconsin and Jim to Michigan,
And then I managed to make two other best friends
One was Mike and the other's name was Jim
Mike and I ate at Lettie's every Tuesday
We worked at Monsanto in Ligonier,
And we planned and took five fishing trips into the wilds of Canada
The excitement was overwhelming as the time to go grew near
My friend Jim also worked at Monsanto
We hunted and partied and fished together,
And one day he gave me a penknife with our names on one side
And the other side was engraved with "friends forever"
Jim and his wife, Barb
Took us on a vacation to Branson,
And the next year was our fiftieth anniversary
And we took them to Yellowstone for some western fun
Shortly after we got back
Cancer took Jim's life away,
A couple months later my wife suffered a devastating stroke
And Mike died in his sleep that very same day
My two best friends were gone
And my wife was paralyzed on her whole right side,
And the stroke also took away her speech
My whole life was scattered to the wind
By the stroke and my two best friends that had just died

I called up one of my classmates
And asked him to pray for us,
And two weeks later
In a car accident he went to be with Jesus
Things just fell apart
With no way to put them back together again,
My wife not being able to walk or talk
And the crushing blow of losing another friend
It was a year after the stroke
Before I could bring my wife home,
I felt so miserable
And so very alone
I took care of her for ten years
Then one day I had a motorcycle accident
That put me in the hospital for five days,
And my wife had to be put in a nursing home
Now I must tell you about God's mysterious ways
I was in the same room with my wife
For over a month of rehab and care,
But all the while that I was recuperating
I wrote many poems, which I shared with the residents there
Jesus always brings the good out of the bad
When your soul seems like a lamp with your wicks growing thin,
And your lamp begins to flicker
It's time to fill it to the full with Jesus again,
Amen

As He Tarries

We must always take the time
To sing God's praises,
And to share his love
All of our God-given days
He has given us life, wonderful life, and more abundant life
And our life has taken on a whole new meaning,
As we our whole lives through walk with him
And in faith in him we keep on leaning
He will never fail us or let us down
And his name shall never pass through our lips taken in vain,
And when we send our prayers up to our Father God
It will always be sent in Christ's most holy and precious name
He answers our prayers
But not always like we think he should,
But he always answers
To bring about the ultimate good
Life is not always
What it's cracked up to be
He is with us on the mountaintop
And he also walks with us through the valley
That day of his glorious and triumphant coming
Is drawing ever so very near,
And we who are washed in the blood of the Lamb
Look forward to that day without dread or fear
On that blessed day we shall rise
And be forever with him,
In that Promised Land that he went to prepare for us
Where dwelleth no sin nor shadows of darkness within

Keeping Our Priorities Straight

When we were young
We dreamed that great treasures would come our way,
Now we rejoice in the little treasures
In our each new day
His blessings
Are all too often overlooked,
And our schedules
Way to overbooked
We need to slow down
And enjoy the good things in life like
Sunny days and refreshing rain
And a loving and devoted wife
He blesses our hearts
Every day,
If we would just go to him
And rejoice with him and pray
He listens to our toils and troubles
He listens to our joys and cares,
And when we reach out to him in faith
He is always there
Don't ever give up
No matter what,
With Jesus by your side
Rejoice for what you've got
Let your treasures be
Of those that are there in heaven,
And he will bless you
More than seventy times seven

Prophesies

The prophesies of old
Are continuing to unfold,
They are consistently and accurately being revealed
Exactly as in the Bible as they were foretold
Some are over and done
And some are yet to come,
And the greatest of them all
Is the coming in the clouds of our Father God, the Creator of Heaven and Earth's Son
This is that long-ago-prophesied event of that long-awaited rapture of the saints
In the twinkling of an eye,
We shall be lifted up to meet Jesus
And go to be with him into that sweet by and by beyond the sky
There will be weeping and gnashing of teeth
For those who are left behind,
Searching for their missing loved ones
Whom they shall never find
The great tribulation shall follow this event
Shortly after the glory of that catching away,
The mark of the beast will be initiated
In all of history, this will be its darkest day
Without that damning mark
You cannot buy or sell,
But if anyone takes that mark
They will be destined for hell
Then after that tribulation comes the binding of Satan for a thousand years
And Christ shall reign on earth as King,
And people will grow like those in the beginning, to live to be very, very old
As all across the earth Christ's peace he will bring

The spears and weapons
Shall be melted down and transformed into plowshares,
The lion will lay down with the lamb
And peace for a thousand years shall lay upon the land
Then Satan shall be loosed to gather his armies
Into the battle of Armageddon,
But it is Jesus who will fight the battle for us
And I read the book and I know who won
Satan and all the fallen angels
And all who have rejected or never accepted Christ,
Those who never took him as Lord and savior
Shall be cast into the lake of fire and outer darkness
A darkness that can be felt where they shall never again see light
This is but a few of the prophesies
But as you live and breathe,
All God's prophesies will come true, and I pray before your eyes close forever on earth
That you come to believe and of Christ's salvation you reach out and receive
I thank you Lord for saving my soul
And for accepting me one day to come and live in your heavenly home,
Thank you for loving me and drawing me to the cross
And for your promise to never forsake or leave me alone
My days I know are few and numbered
And not to be wasted in frivolous pursuits,
I pray that like a mighty oak
You bless me right down to the roots

To God be the glory.

Fields of Harvest

Reach out and touch someone today
You will never know a real blessing
Until you have given one away
There are people all over the world
Who of the gospel message have never heard,
You can make a difference in their lives
With just a smile or an encouraging word
The harvest is truly ready
But the laborers are far too few,
Jesus is asking us to do our part
That means me and you
Of all that we do in his name
He will bless to change their heart,
All he is asking of us
Is that we do our part
It is a privilege and an honor
To be chosen to serve our Lord and King.
And of all in this world that I could ever be
To serve my Lord is the greatest over every other thing

Woolywebster

Brings Back Memories of My Youth

The red barn vividly stands out on Wooly Webster
As does also the Dixie boat painted brightly upon his side,
It makes me glad to call North Webster home
As upon Webster Lake, the rest of my life I intend to abide
My uncles and aunts and my gramma and grampa to
All lived on and around Webster Lake,
And also all my cousins and nieces and nephews and brothers
And others who in and around North Webster planted their stake
I was born in Pierceton, Indiana, in February of 1937
And right after I was born, my father's job took him and us to Seymour,
And that is where I spent the first ten years of my life
I lived the life of a city boy for the entire term of the Second World War
Then, praise the Lord, our family moved back in 1947 to North Webster
This was a paradise to this ten-year-old boy,
It took no time at all in adjusting
As of the surrounding lakes and forests I fully come to love and enjoy
I fished with what I called my magic wand
That long, slender pole called a fly rod,
I put lots of fish on our family's table
And I made more money trapping than if I had gone out and got a job
I hunted those wooded forests
And all across the many a friendly farmer's land,
I camped on islands and in the deep, dark woods
And many other places where many new homes now stand
We cannot turn back the hands of time
And I have great memories of my youth and of this unspoiled wilderness to roam,
I will continue to live in or near North Webster
Till Jesus comes to take me home

Choose You This Day

As Joshua said to the Israelites
Choose you this day whom you will serve,
As for me and mine
We choose the Lord with our hearts clean and pure
Now let me tell you about heaven and hell
And the lengths, breadths, heights, and depths of eternity,
There is a time coming when time shall be no more
A time when we must give account of our lives
To the one yet three of the Holy Trinity
Yes! One day we shall all stand before the judgment seat
And the books shall be opened to reveal our lives therein,
There is another book, the book of life
Those found in this book are those cleansed by the blood of Jesus
Forgiven of all damnation of sin
We all have a choice while we live
To be either going up or down when we die,
Are you going to go down into the fiery pits of hell
Or go up to meet the Lord as he appears in the sky
Hell is a place of darkness, a darkness that can be felt
Where the fire cannot be quenched and where the worm never dies,
Jesus is coming one day for his own
Will you be among the elect as they shout their victory cries?
If you haven't yet given your heart to Jesus
Don't put it off another day,
God has not promised us another tomorrow
Come to Jesus who is the truth, the life, and the way
You will never regret
That step up to the altar of grace,
For no matter what the world throws at you
You have Jesus to see you through every trial that you face

He Is With Us Always

No greater treasure
Shall I ever find,
Than God's gift of poetry
And Jesus to be always on my mind
I'll write until I can write no more
I'll write with the inspiration that God gives to me,
I pray to be known as God's poet, no more and no less,
In these poems, it is God that I want all to see
I want to be an inspiration to others
To use their God-given gifts and talents for Christ's glory,
As they sing, and dance, and play, and work
That others may see Jesus at the center of their life's story
We are but pawns
In the chess game of life,
But in God's eyes
We are crowned to be kings in Christ
As we walk that narrow path
Doing our best in doing God's will
Of all that troubles our hearts in this cruel world
God's wee, small voice speaks these words: "Peace be still"
He is with us always
This is his promise when we came to him,
He is with us wherever we go
There to lead us away from the pathways of sin
He is not only our guide, but he is also our comforter
Through all the trials of life,
With his glorious and forever presence with us
We must always strive to meet life's challenges doing always that which is right

What He's Done for Others

I pray of my life, like the woman that washed Jesus's feet
That I too, have done that which I could,
I pray that my life has meant something to those around me
And that all the bad is outweighed by the good
I am sharing my life with others
Through these verses that I write,
I will never give up hope. And I will keep on running the race
And giving my life here on earth a good fight
Jesus, our trials are hard to understand
As we lay them at your feet,
But we endure those trials like good soldiers of the cross
As you bring about the good out of that which appears to be defeat
Nursing homes are not bad places
They are a place where caring people help others,
Caring for those who cannot care for themselves
Treating them with love, like sisters and like brothers
Yes! Life is hard
In the love of Jesus I live it to the full, one day at a time,
Always taking my joys and my burdens to my Lord
Always praying for his best for answering those prayers of mine
Alice weighs heavy on my heart
As I pray for her every day, along with many others,
I know that God listens
And he knows how much I love her
I am reminded of that beautiful song
Of what he's done for others he will also do for you,
Lord, I pray that you continue to touch our hearts
And continue to prove that song to be true

SEEDS AND WEEDS

We are farmers of a different sort
It is the seeds of life that we sow,
One plants and another waters
But it is Jesus that makes them grow
We plow the furrows
And sow the seeds,
And leave to God
The reaping of the harvest and the sorting out of the weeds
And as that time of Christ's return grows near
I pray that the reapers gather up all that are thine,
We may not be God's chosen people as the Israelites were
But all the same, we are sons and daughters to God, grafted into the vine
The weeds are to be gathered
Gathered together in bundles and burned,
This is their wages, paid in full
That all unrepentant souls have earned
Brothers and sisters in Christ
We are all farmers in a way,
Reaping of that which we have sown
Getting ready for judgment day
Of those who were called and came
Jesus will say "Well done, my good and faithful servants,"
And of the others who just scoffed and turned their backs and walked away
They will be cast into the lake of fire and everlasting torment
Yes! We as farmers
Have faithfully planted the seed,
And all I've got to say is:
Of the coming harvest, don't be a weed

Our Mission

We are saved by grace
Christian is our name,
And when Jesus entered our heart, our whole life began to change
And nothing will ever again be the same
He gave us a new heart
And a new outlook in life,
He gave us a greater purpose
As we stepped out of the darkness and into his glorious light
Life has taken on a whole new meaning
Our lives in him have become a never-ending story.
We have been given newness of life, and like the stars in the heavens
We shall continue forever to shine forth his glory
We shall never have any reason
To walk in self-pity and doubt,
Knowing that our Lord lives within us
And truly and really he is what life is all about
We have placed our souls into his sacred trust
Thanking him for casting away into the wind our every sin,
Trusting in God's sacrificial Lamb
Who totally cleansed us without and within
We know that there is a better place a-waitin'
And in him and through him we can triumphantly face all our trials here,
Knowing that one day we will soon go to be with him
And no one or anything do we need ever fear
We each have a mission placed before us
His mission of reaching out to others,
Of that which God has placed within our hearts
With love and compassion we witness of him to gain new sisters and brothers
God has set this mission before us
His holy mission for us to fulfill,
Born again, filled with joy unspeakable and full of glory
Reaching out with love to others fulfilling in our lives all God's will

Friends and Kin

Keep the heart lamps burning
Filled and forever kindled with the love of Christ
Keeping your feet on the straight and narrow
Always walking in the glory of his everlasting light
Refraining from the lust of the flesh
The pride of life, and the lust of the eyes,
Looking forward to that day of glory
Where in the elect from off the earth shall rise
Free from pain and suffering
Rejoicing with the angels in glory,
Thanking him for drawing us to the cross
Praising him for the victory that lies ahead at the end of our life's story
Oh, to be reunited
With long-ago past friends and kin,
And embrace our loved ones
To hold them in our arms once again
To experience the joy of being in glory
And of seeing Jesus face-to-face,
And to feel the fullness of his love
Praising our Lord for his wondrous gift of saving grace
Angels singing glory to Jesus
As we sing of our joy alongside of them,
And of those of us who were never able to carry a tune before
We will never miss a note in every Jesus-praising hymn
Oh, what joy we have to share
With our loved ones who had gone on before,
Together we will praise our Lord in perfect harmony
Rejoicing in heaven with Jesus forevermore

The Golden Rule

A pine box and a six-foot hole
Life, my friends, does not end in a grave,
It is not what we accumulate out of life
But our eternal joy is of that which we gave
Life is beautiful
And to be lived to the fullest,
But it doesn't mean a thing
If not lived by the golden rule
Do unto others
As you would have them do unto you,
Treat each one like a sister or a brother
And God will add his blessings to all that you undertake to do
Spread the word
Spread the word near and far,
Shine forth his glory
That glory of that of the bright morning star
Witness to the world
Of all that he's done and is still doing for you,
And believe that those blessings that he has bestowed upon you
Will be multiplied many times over in all that you say and do
His eye is on the sparrow
And his watchful eye is also upon me and you,
The world awaits Christ's return
And that promise is ever coming nearer to coming true
Be ready always for the archangel's shout and the trumpet's victorious sound
Sharing the joy of that promise that he made,
And keep the love of Jesus burning in your heart
And never let those flames flicker or fade

In Humble Adoration

In shimmering yellows and reds the leaves of autumn take flight
Joyfully dancing as they tumble down, only to rise up again,
As we in awe are caught up and mesmerized in the glory of it all
The glory of autumn's wondrous colors floating freely in the wind
This is God's season of color that adorns the limbs of the towering trees
This is autumn's awesome wonder taking wing in pastel colors,
God in all his awesome wonder painted and created a masterpiece
A season of awesome beauty unsurpassed by no other
No painter's brush can duplicate the grandeur
Or ever create a more beautiful portrait or ornate picture,
Than that season that God created called autumn
Of colors so bright, brilliant, and pure
We call it fall
Because of the falling leaves,
The glory of God's four seasons
Should touch the unbelievers to open their hearts to believe
Oh, the glory of the stars in the heavens
Oh, the glory of the moon, the sun, the oceans, the seas, and the trees,
All of God's glory that he has laid out before us
Should draw everyone to the cross to bow down upon bended knees
God created all this for us, for us
To cherish and to enjoy,
This is a beautiful world that we live in
And in Genesis is written this account of God's Creation story
With pen and ink, no matter how hard I try
I cannot do justice to God's awesome Creation,
As I write in awe of all that I see
In humble adoration to God in awe and admiration

The Change

We are in an ever-changing world
With a Savior who changes not,
He is the same yesterday, today, and forever
And he promised to be with us always, no matter what
When we first came to believe
When we walked up to the altar of grace,
When we received salvation through Jesus
We received his promise of his going to prepare for us a place
Jesus, come live in our hearts
Come walk with us through life,
Guide us in your footsteps
Clothe us with the whole armor of God
Of which of the enemies of the cross to fight
We have become a new creature of his creation
And he has given each of us a mission to do,
And of all our trials of life
We pray, that side by side with Jesus, he will guide us through
As the trees go through their seasonal changes
So our lives are being changed, dear Jesus, through you,
When we walked up to that altar of grace
We were born again, born to walk this earth anew
Born to live life like it ought to be lived
Born to bring joy into the lives of others,
Born to reach out a helping hand
Born to love one another
Jesus made the difference in our lives
When we accepted his sacrifice for our sin,
Our lives changed forever
That day we gave our heart to him

OF A LOVE SO GRAND

You created the snowflakes
And the beauty of each one differing from one another,
You created the glory of the autumn leaves
And the transformation of their ever-changing color
You created the grandeur of the snowcapped mountains
And the oceans and the seas and all the life therein,
The rivers, the lakes, and the forests
And the sun, the moon, and the stars that never grow dim
You created the rainbow of promise
After the earth was cleansed by the flood,
You created the way of saving grace
By Christ and the cross and his shed blood
Father, you reached out with a love
So wonderful and so grand,
That you would offer up your son
For the reconciliation of fallen man
Jesus, you gave us a way
A way to overcome this world of sin,
You gave us a way to come back
Into your loving arms again
Father, I pray that of all who have come to you,
That they would share their joy of that which is yet to come
And that their lives would be a living testimony of you
In all they say and do in the name of your only begotten son
We pray, give us the words to speak,
Dear Lord, as you guide us in our quest for souls to seek,
Bless us with the infilling of your love
And give us the straight and narrow pathways to guide our Spirit-led feet

The Catching Away

One day, oh, one day
Jesus is going to come and take us home,
One day, oh glorious day
There will be no more of achy breaky of hearts and bone
One day, oh glorious day
We are going to fly away,
We are going to take up wings as eagles
As we leave this world of corruption and decay
When we rise to meet the Lord
The heavenly angels will of our victory sing,
They will rejoice as we rise
Rise to be with our Savior, Lord, and King
Jesus is going to come and take us home
Oh, what a day of rejoicing that will be,
Going home to be with those who have gone on before
Rejoicing together with all the those who have been set free
With open arms
Our kinfolk and friends will welcome us home,
No more pain and no more sorrow
And we will know as we are known
Oh, what a day
Oh, what a wonderful, wonderful day,
A day that will be remembered forever and ever
That day our Lord lifted us up, fulfilling that promise of the catching away
Oh, what a day of rejoicing that is gonna be
Rejoicing with all those who have gone on before,
Oh, what a day, what a glorious, glorious day
When we go to be with Jesus forever and forevermore

I was thinking of Ina when I wrote this poem.

HE IS

One day at a time with Jesus
Is how we must take all that life sends our way,
One day at a time in him we must endure
In faith, trusting in that One to whom we pray
He is our guide through all of our trials of life
In his name we raise our prayers up to our Heavenly Father,
In the name of the One who went to the cross
And shed his blood to cleanse our hearts and make them pure
He is our ever-present loving Savior
Live life to the full in knowing that he is always there,
And when life starts to drag you down
He will bear your heavy-laden burdens as you take them to him in prayer
He is an ever-near help in time of need
He is drawn closer to us through the intercession of prayer,
He is the God of all creation, ever present, always there
Who received us into the open arms of his gentle and loving care
Knowing that he and the father have made their abode in you
Live life, live it in him triumphantly to the very end,
How he can be in you and me and everyone else at the same time
Is more than our finite minds can comprehend
He is everywhere, he is ever present
He is in every living and inanimate thing,
If he was not, all things would cease to be
And the angels would cease to sing
Oh, he is, my friends
He is, and I know that he is,
I've experienced the miracles
The miracles that only he can give
He is our Blessed Redeemer
He is our God, our Lord, and our King,
And if you stop to think about it, he is our everything

Do What You Ought To

All the good that you have ever done,
Is of no avail
Unless it's done in love in the name of God's son
He is the way, the truth, and the life
Only in accepting his sacrifice on the cross,
Will come the peace that passeth all understanding
All other avenues are but dross
Jesus died to set souls free
For all who would come to him,
His blood is the only cure
For the eternal damnation of sin
He is as close as from the pew to the altar,
He is waiting for you to do what you ought to
All that come to him
He will in nowise cast out,
And when you place your soul into his hands
The angels of heaven rejoice and give the victory shout
Everyone dies one day, some
Sooner than others,
Wouldn't you like to go to heaven one day?
Why don't you put that on the top of your list of your druthers?
Read the Bible
Read about his unmerited favor and of all which he has in store,
He will cast your sins as far as the east is from the west
Just come to him and sin no more

BEYOND COMPARE

Set your sights on the Promised Land
And let the world know where you stand,
His is waiting
Waiting to reach out and take you by the hand
If he is knocking on your heart's door,
Open up and let him in,
And let your joy within, to the heavens soar
This world is only a temporary place,
God has better things for us in store
Starting with the blood of the cross and his gift of grace
There is a world of wonder
Beyond our wildest dreams,
In the eternal light of Jesus
The light more glorious than earth's bright and shining of sun beams
Golden streets, an emerald sea of shimmering glass,
Ivory mansions, rainbows, the river of life, the tree of life
And this by no means is all in store for us that he has
Peace, love, joy, and rejoicing in praise to our Lord, God, and King
Lifting up our voices with the angels
In perfect harmony as to him we break forth and sing
In this place of awesome beauty and wonder
This place that is beyond compare,
Just being with loved ones again
Basking in the light and love of Christ and his gentle care

Bejabbers

As I look back upon my life,
Recalling my life's greatest moments
Like the day that I took Alice to be my wife
Then shortly after
There was the arrival of five beautiful girls,
And there ain't nothing prettier
Than little girls with pretty curls
But the greatest day of them all
Was the day that I opened the Bible and the words lifted up off those pages,
That special day was even more special because it was my fortieth birthday
The day that I was introduced to the rock of ages
And instantly he gave me the gift of verse
And as of now, I have seven poem books published and have already written
Another one,
Many miracles I have experienced since I got saved
And I'm looking forward to many more blessings
Before my days on earth are done
A person's whole world changes
When they come to Jesus,
It is so much easier to get through the trials of life
For even into the valleys he will bless
For forty years I walked this earth
With my soul in eternal jeopardy,
And that now scares the bejabbers out of my soul
Knowing now of the dangers that I did not see
I continue to praise the Lord
For my every God-given day,
And my advice to others is this: in all urgency
Make sure of your salvation and of that do not delay

Dancing in the Wind

Snowflakes
Dancing in the wind,
A signaling sign
Of winter about to begin
Hiking along age-old game trails
Through snow-covered pine trees,
Listening to the thunder of ice-splitting cracks
Rumbling across the lakes as they freeze
Sitting down on an old wooden box
Holding a tiny little pole,
Dangling down mousies or hickory nut worms
Through a spudded-out six-inch-width round hole
With shivering shakes
You hover over a Coleman lantern for heat,
Soaking up the warmth
Thawing out frozen hands and feet
Grabbing up old Betsy
As the cold winds blow,
And head out to the woods and fields
Tracking rabbits in the snow
Sitting around the old wood stove
Hypnotized, by the flickering flames,
Watching old movies
Trying to remember the actors' names
Don't let cabin fever shut you in
Get out every chance you can,
And enjoy every God-given day of the best of every season
That ever-changing transformation that's taking place all across the land

Thanksgiving Is Every Day

It is Thanksgiving time
Time to count our many blessings,
Like food on the table and warm clothes on our back
And many other wonderful things
A place to call home
Oh, the joy to be living in a God-loving country,
Sharing our love of Jesus with others
Continually rejoicing in this land of the brave, the bold, and the free
This country is of thee O Lord our God
And you have left it up to us to keep it that way,
We must keep you always in our hearts
And of those who defend this country we must never cease to pray
We pray for the churches throughout the land
And all those who are preaching and reaching out,
We must uphold the ministers of the written word who feed the flock
And ourselves continue to witness, for that is what Christianity is all about
This country would not be
The country that it is,
This country is God's country
Because within our hearts he lives
We must thank him every day
And not just on Thanksgiving Day,
We must thank him for all the good that he has done
And all the blessings that he has sent our way
Truly we are blessed
What a savior who took our sins to bear, nailing them to the cross,
Without him and his sacrifice our souls, our country,
And our freedom, would be forever lost
Praise God through whom all blessings flow

The Day Our Savior Drew Near

Christmas is the time for the joy of giving
And a time of thankfulness for that which we receive,
It is a holy day of joy and hope
Touching hearts to overflowing with love to all who believe
The day that the Christ child was born
The day that the Virgin Mary gave birth,
The day our Savior left his home in glory
To dwell as a man upon his creation of Mother Earth
God created a miracle in the heavens of a wondering star
To hover over and shine down upon our Savior lying in the manger below,
This same star was to guide the magi of the east
To that sacred place where they were divinely destined by God to go
The Savior came down to earth
To reinstate man back to spiritual health again,
To give his life blood upon that old rugged cross
Carrying upon himself all our condemnation of sin
Unmerited favor
Something more wonderful than money could ever buy,
Saving grace
Of which with tears of joy we shout the victory cry
There is nothing that we could ever do
To merit this gift that God has given,
Except accept with all our heart and soul
All that he has done to make our lives through him worth livin'
Christmas is the most looked-forward-to day
Of all the holidays of the year,
It is the day of the virgin birth
The day our Savior drew near

CROSSING OVER

A new year with a new beginning
Filled with joy and hope within,
As we receive God's promise
Of life without end
We take one day at a time
As we walk in our Savior's footsteps,
Traveling the upward road to glory
To one day leave this world with no regrets
We go to receive our new home
And a new body that never grows old,
In a place more beautiful
That the fullness thereof could never be told
Walk the hallelujah trail
Walk it till the end of time,
Walk it into eternity
Where love is the tie that binds
Jesus awaits with open arms
To welcome us into his heavenly home
Forget those treasures that you leave behind,
For the treasures in heaven are far greater
Than here on earth that you could ever find
He will shower you with love
As you rejoice with the holy angels in praise and song,
With all thoughts of this corrupt world
Now and forever gone
There's a better place a-waitin'
On that far and distant shore,
Ain't a-gonna need this house no longer
Ain' t a-gonna need this house no more

Be Not Silent

I love my Jesus
And he loves me in spite of my faults,
I will never forget the cross
And the price for which my freedom was bought
O Lord of the moon and stars
O Lord of heaven and earth,
You paid the ultimate price
For what you deemed a soul's worth
It is now our turn to do our part
Of leading others to the cross,
His goal is that through us and our testimony
That none be lost
Believe and be baptized
And go and spread the Living Word,
A silent Christian is a dead Christian
Let the word from the depths of your soul be heard
We are to carry on
Doing what Christ began to do,
We are his spokespersons here on earth
Laborers of the harvest and way too few
He has set a goal for us
To reach out to the ends of the earth,
And in our heart of hearts we need to show Jesus
What we deem a soul is worth

Blessed Assurance

If you've got Jesus in your heart
Do not hold him within yourself,
Jesus is not a trophy
To be left collecting dust upon a shelf
Announce to the world
That the Lord has come,
And that within you
Lives God's only begotten son
We can now face the world
With a new outlook in life,
For within us lives
The Lord of Life, the Blessed Messiah, Jesus Christ
There is no other fount I know
Whereby to cleanse one's soul,
Only the blood of Jesus
Can make one whole
Come give your life to him
Who gave his life for you,
And discover a world more beautiful
Of skies more gloriously blue
When we look at this world
Through the eyes of Jesus,
We will discover the need of telling others
What Jesus has done for us
He gave his life
To save lost souls,
Then he took up his life again
To assure us of our eternal goal

Wings as Eagles

One day the graves of the saved will be opened
When Christ appears on high,
And we who are alive in Christ shall be lifted up with them
To meet our Lord in the sky
To a city not made with human hands
Glowing with streets of gold,
No sun, no moon, for the Lord is the light thereof
Streets lined with ivory palaces and an emerald sea of glass, so I'm told
No more pain, heartaches, nor sorrows
Our families rejoined, back together again,
Singing with the angels the old hallelujah songs
And rejoicing together with long-ago past friends
We shall take up wings as eagles
We shall rejoice on high with the saints,
We shall run and not be weary
And we shall walk and not faint
A place of wonder beyond all imaginations
A place of tranquil peace,
Oh, to be on that other shore
Where all our earthly troubles cease
With undying faith we must believe
Compared to eternity this world is but a passing moment,
We must live our lives sharing our Jesus's joy
Sharing the age-old story of the babe who was heaven-sent
Faith is the substance of things hoped for
Faith is what moves the mountains,
Faith in believing is what draws us to the altar of grace
And the river of life's ever-flowing fountain

Home Sweet Home

The church bells are ringing
The congregations are singing,
There is a melody in the air
Cold hearts are changing
With smiles upon their faces
Souls are inviting Jesus in,
His death on the cross was not in vain
His shed blood still has the power to wash away sin
Praises to Jesus
Are still being lifted up to the heaven of heavens,
More and more souls are coming to kneel at the altar
Opening their hearts to let the Lord of Life come in
A revival is taking place,
Souls reaching out
To receive God's gift of amazing grace
Oh, what wonderful poems
That the Lord has placed in my heart,
So many beautiful and wonderful thoughts
I sometimes don't know where to start
Above and beyond this world
Lies a place of beauty and wonder
A place beyond description
A place for which we continually hunger
When Jesus came into our hearts
He promised that we would never again be alone,
And one day, oh yes, one glorious day
He's coming back to take us home

CHRISTIANS INDEED

I don't need tobacco or alcohol
I don't run around and I'm not given to cuss
I'm pushing eighty
And all I ever need or want is Jesus
I'm short on money
But I'm long on God's blessings,
I pray one day
To join the angels in joyous singing
We have a mission here on earth to fulfill
As long as we have the breath of life,
And that is to reach out to the world and share God's message of forgiveness
Purchased upon the cross by Jesus Christ
There are many who have never heard
Of God's Good News of saving grace,
Too many are going down the wrong paths
Too many who have a horrible eternity to face
We as Christians
Are to share our Jesus joy,
We are to draw others in
By faithfully sharing the gospel story
Life is not just about surviving
It's about reaching out to others,
It is about making for Christ's kingdom of glory
New sisters and new brothers
If we are going about doing what needs to be done
Then and only then are we Christians indeed,
Spreading the gospel message in words and deeds
Planting for the coming harvest of God's life-giving seed

All That Matters

Keep on keeping on, following that bright and morning star
That wondrous star that leads to the Promised Land,
No other paths dare a Christian walk
Who has for Jesus firmly made his stand
One day at a time is how we face life's many trials
As we walk with Jesus upon this temporal terrestrial planet we now call home,
We've come to realize that we cannot make it to heaven on our own
And that the paths that he has set before us, we do not walk alone
He is the Bread of Life
He is the Living Waters,
He is the King of Kings
And he is ours, and that is all that matters
When we walk through the valley of the shadow of death
We will fear no evil upon our soul,
For our Jesus lives and walks with us
And he ensures us of our final destination's goal
He is the light
The light that outshines the sun,
He is the shadowless light of heaven's far-off domain
He is the Holy One whereby upon the cross our victory was won
No other path will we follow
We will not let anything deter us from our eternal destiny,
We have put our souls into our Savior's hands
Those hands for us that was nailed to a tree
He is our joy and our happiness
He is our ever-present guide,
Without him we would be forever lost
He lived and died and rose to life again and walks forever by our side

About the Author

Thomas Kruger turned eighty years old in February. He lives on Webster Lake and is an avid fly fisherman and loves the great outdoors. Right now, he spends every day from 9:30 a.m. to 4:00 p.m. at the Oaks Nursing Home in Columbus City to visit his wife. She is a resident there due to having a stroke ten years ago, and cannot talk and is paralyzed on the right side. But her brain is still sharper than Thomas's. Praise God that she is still among the living.